Likewise in Life

Life Lessons from the Playing Field

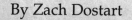

By Zach Dostart

All scripture references are from the New International Version Bible, CD-ROM, © 1999 by Zondervan Publishing, Inc. unless otherwise noted.

Published in San Diego, USA
by Top Shelf Publishing,4370 La Jolla Village Drive, Suite 970, San Diego, USA.

Library of Congress Cataloging-in-Publication Data: 2002116018

ISBN No. 0-932766-68-4

Printed in the United States of America

This book began as a series of conversations my Dad and I had over breakfast. Naturally, we talked about sports. Dad would ask me about the previous day's practice or what I had learned from a game situation. We talked a lot about winning and losing, attitude and dedication, commitment and sportsmanship.

While I was in eighth grade, Dad suggested I write down the key points of our breakfast conversations in my journal. After my junior year, I assembled those breakfast notes into the pages of this book.

Zach Dostart
La Jolla High School

Fathers are not called to be their child's best friend. We are called to praise and admonish, to instruct, to identify values, and to serve as a role model in daily life. Zach has taught me a great deal about sports over the past several years. I hope and believe Zach has learned valuable life lessons as well.

By the way, Zach's high school athletics ended up on a high note. In June 2000, Zach was named a lacrosse All American. I know he will do likewise in life.

Paul Dostart
La Jolla, California

Dedication

This book is dedicated to Joyce Dostart and to Sam Dostart.

Without their love, support and encouragement,

this book would not have been possible.

ndure hardship with us like a good soldier of Christ Jesus. No one serving as a soldier gets involved in civilian affairs—he wants to please his commanding officer. Similarly, if anyone competes as an athlete, he does not receive the victor's crown unless he competes according to the rules.

2 Timothy 2:3-5

The Purpose of Sports

American Indians invented the game of lacrosse to train their braves to be tough. It was a form of military training. The lives of the braves, and possibly the whole tribe, depended upon the fitness of the braves. They played lacrosse as a game, but it was played to prepare the braves for battle—to defend the lives of the tribe.

Likewise in Life. Today's battle is trying to gain the competitive edge in business. The person who develops a habit of physical fitness, focus, teamwork and competition when he is young, will become the successful adult.

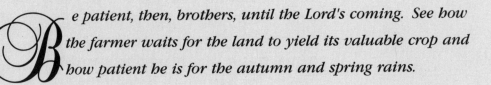

e patient, then, brothers, until the Lord's coming. See how the farmer waits for the land to yield its valuable crop and how patient he is for the autumn and spring rains.

James 5:7

They Only Remember the Final Score

One of the best lessons I learned playing sports is that you can lose a lot and still win. A soccer team may bring the ball down the field 30 times during a game, but only score twice. When the game is won 2-1, no one remembers the 28 times the team tried to score and failed.

Likewise in Life. Many opportunities will arise in a lifetime. It is important to make many attempts, for those who do will have a better chance of success. Make the attempt. Risk. Although many attempts may fail, the ones that succeed will carry the day.

reate in me a pure heart, O God, and renew a steadfast spirit within me.

Psalms 51:10

Be Ready

The team's best player will get sick or injured at some time. Practice hard daily, stay motivated, and you will be ready for any situation. With true effort and hardiness the law of averages will follow.

Likewise in Life. The opportunity to pitch the big account could come at any time. Have your presentation ready, your shoes shined, and be dressed to sell. Your chance for success increases if you are ready.

Don't Forget to Run

Charlie is on my baseball team. He can hit the ball better than most of the guys on our team, but Charlie's batting average is the lowest on the team. Sometimes, after one of his leather-tearing hits, Charlie forgets to run. He stays at the plate, watching the path of the ball. To improve his batting average, Charlie must run for first as soon as he connects.

Likewise in Life. It is not enough merely to take a swing by pitching a sale. You still have to follow up—run the bases—and complete what you started to achieve true success.

veryone who competes in the games goes into strict training. They do it to get a crown that will not last; but we do it to get a crown that will last forever.

1 Corinthians 9:25

Practice Makes Permanent

Practicing your shot is crucial, but proper practice is essential. Practice imprints an action into your brain. Anyone can practice repeatedly—the wrong way. Your body repeats the action your brain has learned. The way you practice is just as important as how often you practice.

Likewise in Life. Habits are formed from repeated conduct. So, practice doing things right and with good effort each time. All your actions will then repeat the conduct you have rehearsed. Consistent, exemplary conduct leads to a habit of success.

We also rejoice in our sufferings, because we know that suffering produces perseverance; perseverance, character; and character, hope. And hope does not disappoint us, because God has poured out his love into our hearts by the Holy Spirit, whom he has given us.

Romans 5:3-5

The Longest Walk

After striking out you must walk back to your teammates in the dugout. Some have called this the longest walk in the world, but it can be a powerful teacher. Learning to fail individually, while winning as a team, is a big life lesson.

Likewise in Life. Everyone suffers losses. Strive to gain the perspective that some losses are inevitable stepping stones on the path to success.

o not neglect your gift.... Be diligent in these matters; give yourself wholly to them, so that everyone may see your progress.

1 Timothy 4:14-15

Become Good At It

Nobody likes to play a sport he is not good at. On the other hand, you cannot get good if you do not practice. Sticking with a sport and having plenty of proper practice invariably develops skill. Suddenly, the sport becomes fun.

Likewise in Life. Everyone experiences a learning curve in any new situation, but consistent, hard work and effort lead to outstanding performance and, eventually, enjoyment of a job well done.

He gives strength to the weary and increases the power of the weak. Even youths grow tired and weary, and young men stumble and fall; but those who hope in the Lord will renew their strength. They will soar on wings like eagles; they will run and not grow weary, they will walk and not be faint.

Isaiah 40:29-30

Learn To Play Midfield

In lacrosse and soccer the midfielders do most of the running. If you train to be a 'middie' by doing a lot of running, then you can be an attacker if ever the need arises. But, if you only train to play attack, it will be hard to be a middie because you will not have the endurance.

Likewise in Life. To rise to the top, taking only 'cush' jobs will not cut it. Preparation in a more arduous position will enable you to succeed more rapidly.

or physical training is of some value, but godliness has value for all things, holding promise for both the present life and the life to come.

1 Timothy 4:8

Be In It For The Long Term

When you are nine years old, all you need is a general athletic ability to be a competitive player. By the time you are 15 or 16 years old, you need that ability plus a specific skill in the game itself. Just being athletic is now not enough. In those seven short years, about 80% of the participants will drop out.

Likewise in life. Any person who rises to the top of his or her profession does so by competing over the long term, acquiring specific skills, and constantly striving to improve.

Therefore encourage one another and build each other up, just as in fact you are doing. Now we ask you, brothers, to respect those who work hard among you, who are over you in the Lord and who admonish you.

1 Thessalonians 5:11-12

The Perfect Game

Some people think the perfect game is achieved only by striking out every batter, but that is not true. Even a 3-up, 3-down performance for nine innings, requires a minimum of 81 pitches, and there are few pitchers good enough to strike out 27 batters. The same no-hit shutout happens when a solid defense allows no one to reach first. The perfect-game pitcher does not have to be perfect with every pitch.

Likewise in Life. By building a team that supports all your efforts, you can still succeed on an 'off' day. You can do it with one-third the work, and you do not have to be perfect. Strive for perfection, but build a team that allows you to be human.

God has arranged the parts in the body, every one of them, just as he wanted them to be. If they were all one part, where would the body be? As it is, there are many parts, but one body... those parts of the body that seem to be weaker are indispensable...

1 Corinthians 12:18-22

Every Member Contributes

Once in a while you see a team with a few players scoring most of the points. But even the teammates who do not score are important to the team. Without the defenders, there would not be a team, and the players who score would not have the chance to score, or even play.

Likewise in Life. One employee may close most of the deals that bring the company large contracts. While this person may be important, without the other people in the company contributing, it probably would not have been possible.

I will instruct you and teach you in the way you should go; I will counsel you and watch over you... the Lord's unfailing love surrounds the man who trusts in him.

Psalms 32:8-10

Concentrate

At lacrosse camp we do three 3-hour practice sessions per day, with each coach instructing about six players. In such a regime, we quickly learn game skills. After school practices teach some skills, but mostly teamwork. Concentrated instruction is the best way to develop superior individual skills.

Likewise in Life. When you focus on the fundamentals in a concentrated fashion, you develop skills quickly. Using those skills daily brings success for the whole team.

CHALLENGE!

My extremely emotional soccer coach was always urging us to "Challenge!" the opposing player. When we did it, we soon shifted from being on defense to being on offense. As a result, we ended up both seasons undefeated.

Likewise in Life. Being a consistent competitor in business is important. By always challenging your competition, and yourself, you increase profits. Once you ease off, the competition has a chance to catch up and push right past you.

isten to advice and accept instruction. In the end you will be wise.

Proverbs 19:20

Learn to Listen

Listening to a coach is a crucial part of being a great player. Following directions is an asset every player must have. Great coaching is wasted if a player will not listen.

Likewise in Life. Business mentors are available to those willing to listen. Those nearing retirement are glad to share their wisdom. Libraries are filled with tomes outlining the pathway to achievement. Audiotapes are available with tips and techniques on any subject. A willingness to listen demonstrates a desire to learn.

...since we have such a hope, we are very bold.

2 Corinthians 3:12

Risky or Reckless?

When the defense stays tight under the basket, the team feeds its best 3-point shooter for two reasons: 1) He might score a 3-pointer and, 2) his attempts will pull the defense out and open up the center for the rest of the team. The 3-pointer is a low-percentage shot, but the potential reward justifies the bigger risk.

Likewise in Life. It's OK to attempt a higher risk alternative when lower risk options are not working. A calculated risk will achieve more if it succeeds. Think it through. Impulsive actions are reckless and do more harm than good. Take the risks, but don't be reckless.

...to the pure, show yourself pure. To the crooked, you show yourself shrewd.

Psalms 18:26

Do It Again

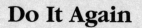

Suppose the defender covering you can be out maneuvered by faking left and then going right. If it worked once on him—try it again. Some people do not analyze their mistakes.

Likewise in Life. Many successes come by 'out thinking' the competition. A winning strategy can be used again until it no longer works. Be alert to that moment. Then try something new.

For everything that was written in the past was written to teach us, so that through endurance and the encouragement of the Scriptures we might have hope.

Romans 15:4

Learn From Your Mistakes

Midway through the school year, and again at the end, there are big tests that re-cap everything studied. You must review previous quizzes and study from your mistakes.

Likewise in Life. Learning from the past is crucial to success in business. Most millionaires are rich from hard work and the determination to learn from their mistakes. The biggest mistake the men of today make is not learning from the mistakes of yesterday.

So do not throw away your confidence; it will be richly rewarded. You need to persevere so that when you have done the will of God, you will receive what he has promised.

Hebrews 10:35-36

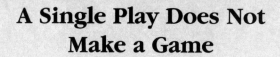

A Single Play Does Not Make a Game

When you watch the highlights of any game you view a series of four-second clips. What really happened was a two-hour contest, filled with not-so-spectacular plays.

Likewise in Life. Though winning the big contract may get attention, remember that every big event is the culmination of a series of diligent, behind the scenes' efforts.

Each one should use whatever gift he has received to serve others, faithfully administering God's grace in its various forms. If anyone speaks, he should do it as one speaking the very words of God. If anyone serves, he should do it with the strength God provides, so that in all things God may be praised through Jesus Christ.

1 Peter 4:10-11

Natural Athletes Are Made, Not Born

We all talk of 'natural' athletes, and it does seem that some people have a special knack for certain things. But it was not always so—even for those 'natural' athletes. Ask their fathers and mothers; at some point they were as clumsy as their friends. What happened in between was training. Long hours of time on task, hard work, muscle memory... and 'suddenly' a natural athlete is born.

Likewise in Life. Good salesmen study top selling techniques. Great surgeons practice to acquire acute skills. Winning trial lawyers rehearse their arguments. In every vocation, the top talent got there by focused hard work and time dedicated to the task.

ut I will come to you very soon, if the Lord is willing, and then I will find out not only how these arrogant people are talking, but what power they have. For the kingdom of God is not a matter of talk, but of power.

1 Corinthians 4:19-20

Show Them
What You Can Do

Michael Jordan is probably the greatest basketball player—ever. At one time, people whispered he was getting too old, afraid to drive hard to the basket. In February 1997, the head coach of the Seattle Supersonics voiced those whispers aloud just prior to a game against the Bulls. Jordan answered him with 48 points of his own, leading to a huge win over the Supersonics.

Likewise in Life. Confidence in yourself and your abilities needs to come from within. Otherwise people's negative talk can easily defeat you. Do not tell them what you can do, show them.

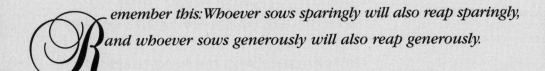

*R*emember this: Whoever sows sparingly will also reap sparingly, and whoever sows generously will also reap generously.

2 Corinthians 9:6

500 Grounders a Week

Baseball season begins. It's time to field some grounders. Take a bucket of balls, a bat, and a friend to the park. Stand in front of the fence and field ten buckets of grounders. In the average game you will field less than 10 grounders. You will see 50 times that number after a week of ten buckets a day in the park.

Likewise in Life. The one who is willing to invest the time developing a skill, is the one who will not choke at the crucial moment. A confident, competent person inspires others to excel.

e strong and courageous. Do not be terrified; do not be discouraged, for the LORD your God will be with you wherever you go.

Joshua 1:9

The Fastest Game
On Two Feet

Running is the main part of the game of lacrosse. The ball moves very fast and hardly ever stops. The lesson of lacrosse is never to give up. Even after a player beats you to the ball, turn around and chase him. You have a 50/50 chance of catching him and winning the ball.

Likewise in Life. There will be times when someone beats you fair and square. These are the times to show that you do not accept losing. Be determined enough to review the loss. Make the necessary improvements or corrections that will keep that loss the only one of its kind.

Don't Lose Hope

A running back fumbles. Every player on the field wants possession of the ball. The competitor who continues to go after the ball even after it may seem impossible, will end up recovering the fumble.

Likewise in Life. You made your best sales pitch, and the customer decides to go with another company. Do not lose hope. The other company may drop the ball, allowing you to make that sale yet.

You are the light of the world. A city on the hill cannot be hidden. Neither do people light a lamp and put it under a bowl....

Matthew 5:14-15

Find Your Gift and Use It

A high school kid decides to not go out for football next year. This would be a loss, but it will open new doors. If not football then basketball, if not athletics, then as a matter of personal growth, he should develop his abilities in computers, in art, in music, or wherever his talent may lie.

Likewise in Life. When you use your abilities in different situations, you increase the chance of your special gift being revealed to you. Using that gift to your best potential is what separates the winners from the losers.

lessed is the man who perseveres under trial, because when he has stood the test, he will receive the crown of life that God has promised to those who love him.

James 1:12

Big Potatoes Rise to the Top

Potato farmers know that larger potatoes fetch a higher price. So, when the potatoes are ready for market, the farmer drives his wagon down the bumpiest road. The farmer knows the largest potatoes rise to the top on a bumpy road.

Likewise in Life. Strong character develops during 'bumpy' experiences. Big people, like big potatoes, will learn to thrive on bumpy experiences as their character grows. Indeed, just as the farmer follows the bumpy road, you should gratefully accept any setbacks as character-building experiences. They help you rise to the top in your wagon of life.

nd let us not grow weary in doing good, for at the proper time we will reap a harvest, if we do not give up.

Galatians 6:9

Structure and Discipline Fuel Creative Thinking

Some people think that creativity comes from 'no boundaries' and 'no limits.' But in fact, most creative people have both structure and discipline. Great coaches prepare for contests by developing a game plan that capitalizes on his team's strengths while exploiting the opponent's weaknesses. People will call him creative, not realizing that his excellent play calling was born from hours of planning.

Likewise in Life. Creative people approach their work in a methodical and self-disciplined fashion. Writers write every day. Musicians practice scales for hours so they can improvise with ease. Even the so-called 'free thinkers' spend hours finding different ways to accomplish the same task.

Your strength will be spent in vain, because your soil will not yield its crops, nor will the trees of the land yield their fruit.

Leviticus 26:20

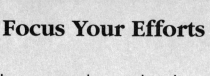

Focus Your Efforts

The soccer player who chases the ball all over the field may be showing tremendous effort, but is abandoning his assigned position. Undisciplined players must be pulled out of the game, or the whole team will suffer.

Likewise in Life. The employee who extends great effort in too many areas at once will achieve few results. The rewards of success go to those who understand their specific role and focus their efforts.

im for perfection, listen to my appeal, be of one mind, live in peace. And the God of love and peace will be with you.

2 Corinthians 13:11

Specialize

As you get older, time pressures dictate that you limit your time to one or two sports, instead of three or four. As children grow up, they play many sports. This is good for them because they learn many things, including commitment and leadership. As the child gets older, it is important to focus their efforts. If an athlete plays a sport in every season; there is little time for homework, and no off-season to train.

Likewise in Life. The rookie in every company should learn all of the departments. However, if you want to move up the corporate ladder, you must narrow your focus, and sharpen your skills.

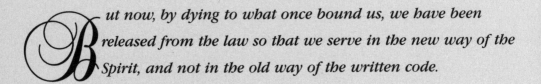

But now, by dying to what once bound us, we have been released from the law so that we serve in the new way of the Spirit, and not in the old way of the written code.

Romans 7:6

Know When to Quit

There comes a time when a sport no longer holds the allure it once did. When you are the last in the batting order, odd numbered innings in right field, or you always sit on the bench, you are not gaining ground. Finish the season to be respectful to your coach and teammates, and begin a new sport next year. When the end of the season is too far away, move on.

Likewise in Life. When, after years of constant hard work, the promotion you deserve is not coming, it is time to leave. Quitting too soon is a bad habit, but quitting to get a better beginning can sometimes be the best decision.

The Sovereign Lord is my strength he will make my feet like deer's feet, and he enables me to go on the heights.

Habakkuk 3:19

Hustle!

Most athletes agree that even the weakest player on the team can contribute something by hustling. Hustling wins games. Hustling is diving for an out-of-bounds ball, sprinting down the court to get back on defense, 'boxing out' and playing with enthusiasm. The hustle someone shows does not show how fast he can run or even how long he can run. It shows how big his heart is.

Likewise in Life. Someone may have more work experience or better connections, but with hustle—working harder and smarter—you can be a valued member of a winning business team.

Trust in the Lord with all your heart and lean not on your own understanding, in all your ways acknowledge him and he will make straight your paths.

Proverbs 3:5-6

V-Cut – A Simple Way to Get Open

In most team ball games, a player can shake a defender and get open by using a 'V-Cut.' In a V-Cut, you move towards the goal, then cut back towards the ball. Your defender will move with you towards the goal; his own momentum will move him past you, leaving you wide open for the pass. Using a V-Cut to deflect your defender can give your teammates a chance to go to the goal.

Likewise in Life. The challenges we face in life are like the defenders in a ball game. To shake off a challenger, make a move toward your goal—if unopposed, seize it. If you are opposed, "V-Cut" in a different direction and try again.

*t is fine to be zealous, provided the purpose is good....*

Galatians 4:18

Stay Involved

No matter how good your skills are, if winning is your goal, you must play like a winner. Every player must play as if everything he does is important to the success of the team. Even sitting on the bench, a player should be attentive to the game, using the time to analyze the opponents. Every player must be in the game, if not physically, then mentally.

Likewise in Life. Even if you are not the one making the presentation today, go ready to give it. Look interested. Be interested. You might be surprised by what you learn...or what you are called upon to do.

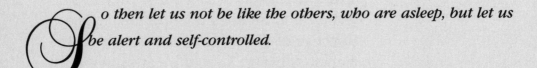

So then let us not be like the others, who are asleep, but let us be alert and self-controlled.

Galatians 5:6

Scan the Field

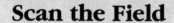

    In every sport you must know what is happening on the playing field. Plays develop, creases open, and scoring opportunities appear. It is impossible to see these things if you are not constantly looking around, scanning the field.

    Likewise in Life. Opportunities to land a sale, to propose a novel idea, or to grab a promotion come and go quickly. Be alert to your environment at all times and you will be rewarded.

TEAM = Together Everyone Achieves More

Many basketball teams have a 'ball hog'. This person is usually not a bad player, but hogging the ball pits him against his own teammates. Ball hogs do not help the team. They are playing for individual statistics. If everyone passes the ball and contributes to the team, more baskets are made, increasing the chances for a win.

Likewise in Life. Opportunities to help others will arise often. When they do, help your friends and associates. A time will come when you need help and your example will teach your others how to reciprocate.

If you put away the sin that is in your hand and allow no evil to dwell in your tent, then you will lift up your face without shame; you will stand firm and without fear. You will surely forget your trouble, recalling it only as waters gone by.

Job 11:14-16

Time-Out

In basketball, and many other sports, time-outs are called. Time-outs have many purposes. Some coaches call time-outs when their team is confused and struggling. Other coaches call time-outs when the opposite team is doing well. It can make them lose their momentum. Time-outs allow coaches and players to re-group and get back in the game. Time-outs are a critical element of most games.

Likewise in Life. Occasionally things will stop going your way. Step back and take time to assess the situation. Figure out what needs to be changed, make the adjustment and begin anew.

e very careful, then, how you live—not as unwise but as wise, making the most of every opportunity....

Ephesians 5:15

Convert the Free Throws

There are fouls in every game. Some fouls lead to free throws. It is important for each player to show up for the game prepared to convert a free throw into a point if the opportunity is presented. Often, missed free throws can account for the difference between a winning and loosing score.

Likewise in Life. The wise business person prepares for the occasional 'free throw' opportunity. If a big competitor closes his factory for renovation and all his customers temporarily come to you, how many will you retain when the competitor reopens?

e prepared in season and out of season; correct, rebuke and encourage—with great patience and careful instruction....

2 Timothy 4:2

Plan Your Work;
Work Your Plan

Strategy is very important.
Preparation is a critical factor in any contest.
To prepare, scout the competition, develop
a game plan, and begin each game ready
to win.

*Likewise in Life. Making an effective
presentation requires careful preparation
and a well-thought out plan. Contracts
usually come from knowing your competition
and proving that your company is the
expert in its field.*

I appeal to you, brothers, in the name of our Lord Jesus Christ, that all of you agree with one another so that there may be no divisions among you and that you may be perfectly united in mind and thought.

1 Corinthians 1:10

Every Member, Every Minute

A basketball team has five players. If one of the players is physically on the floor but mentally out of the game, the odds of winning have shifted to the team playing with all 5 players fully engaged. When the forwards are rebounding the ball, the guard who is not already looking for a break is handicapping his team.

Likewise in Life. Business depends on teams—fully engaged—to be successful. If team members are not contributing equally, the entire team, possibly the company, suffers when a deadline is missed or the contract is not signed. Everyone pulling together can make the difference between success and failure.

*ever be lacking in zeal, but keep your spiritual fervor,
serving the Lord. Be joyful in hope, patient in affliction,
faithful in prayer.*

Romans 12:11-12

Play to Win

The team which is ahead at half-time usually wins the game. If they have a large lead, it is nearly impossible to come back. Therefore, do not 'pace your-self' but go all out from the very start. If you gain a commanding lead, the other players can maintain it while you rest.

Likewise in Life. The person who gives his all to an entry-level job will be rapidly promoted. After consistent hard work, when you need a 'pause' (to be married or have a baby) the team and the momentum you have built up will ensure no ground is lost.

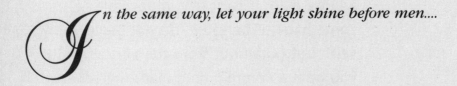

In the same way, let your light shine before men....

Matthew 5: 16

Show Them Your Best

Many try out for high school basket-ball teams. Oddly, some players with good skills are cut by not showing their best attributes, or—worse—showing the wrong ones. Showing up at every practice, and giving 100% effort all the time are qualities that impress coaches. There is also leadership, sportsmanship and coachability. Coaches look for these traits when picking the team.

Likewise in Life. First impressions are powerful—and immediate. Bad first impressions are hard to 'undo'. When you reveal your best traits right away, you are more likely to experience a positive response—and success—immediately.

ommit the Lord whatever you do and your plans will succeed.

Proverbs 16:3

The Thinking Man's Game

Strategy in baseball is deliberate and well thought out, despite the slow pace of the game. If played well, baseball is a game in which every move is part of an overall plan. It takes a wise manager to make all the right moves that score runs.

Likewise in Life. The wise person will make decisions that build for the future. The ones who think ahead will finish ahead, for they always have their next move in mind.

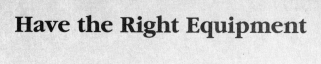

Have the Right Equipment

You are setting yourself up for mediocrity if you use mediocre equipment. Inferior equipment compromises months of training.

Likewise in Life. A superior product or service is the outcome of superior input. Inferior input cheapens the product and lessens its effectiveness, and value, in the marketplace.

nd do not forget to do good and to share with others, for with such sacrifices God is pleased.

Hebrews 13:16

Give Away the Ball

There are always players who try to take the ball and score themselves. This type of player is usually not helping the team win. A team that plays unselfishly will probably beat any team whose game plan is to have only one person score.

Likewise in Life. Some employees think only their efforts are the key to success of the company. While some may be 'stars,' the people who learn to work together as a team are more successful. Teamwork benefits everyone. Together Everyone Achieves More.

ince an overseer is entrusted with God's work, he must be blameless—not overbearing, not quick-tempered, not given to drunkenness, not violent, not pursuing dishonest gain. Rather he must be hospitable, one who loves what is good, who is self-controlled, upright, holy and disciplined.

Titus 1:7

Positive Coaching

There are coaches who spend all their time yelling. Usually they yell because their teams are not doing well. Coaches need to be positive and supportive to help players develop proper skills. The best coaches put the focus on the conduct they want to see.

Likewise in Life. The team leader who focuses his efforts only on embarrassing and taunting his colleagues is destructive and creates a low-performing, no-morale team. The leader who focuses on positive behavior and who praises good performances gets just that—and a motivated group!

n attacker advances against you. Guard the fortress, watch the road, brace yourselves, marshal all your strength!

Nahum 2:1

Be an Effective Threat

To be effective in basketball the person with the ball must maintain a position called the triple threat. This position allows the player to pass, shoot or dribble with ease. Opposing players see him as a threat, and accord him respect.

Likewise in Life. The person with options will earn the respect of his colleagues and competitors. The person who can easily land a better job somewhere else will be much more likely to get a raise at his current job.

I lift up my eyes to the hills—where does my help come *from?* My help comes from the Lord, the Maker of heaven and *earth.* He will not let your foot slip—he who watches over you will not slumber.

Psalm 121:1-3

Keep Your Head Up

In basketball, the person with the ball must be ready to pass it away at all times. If you dribble with your head down, you will not see the court ahead, or the obvious pass. In sports, it is important to keep your head up.

Likewise in Life. Whether you own your own business or work for a huge corporation, it is important to be aware of what is going on within the business. By 'keeping your head up' you will see what is ahead and be ready for a fast-breaking opportunity.

bey your leaders and submit to their authority. They keep watch over you as men who must give an account. Obey them so that their work will be a joy, not a burden, for that would be of no advantage to you.

Hebrews 13:17

Turning Coal into Diamonds

The good coach applies a lot of pressure to teach his players. Coaches push players to give total effort throughout the game, and stay mentally focused. Coaches, for the most part, decide when to substitute, call time outs, or try a new play. Many people blame coaches for an underachieving team. If the talent is there, the good coach can develop a winning team.

Likewise in Life. Good supervisors are driven to produce a successful team. Supervisors know how to apply positive pressure so their employees work harder while doing their best work.

Everyone should be quick to listen, slow to speak and slow to become angry, for man's anger does not bring about the righteous life that God desires.

James 1:19-20

Practice Self-Control

It is common in basketball to elbow and push the other player, or say things to goad him. This is part of the game. These little things do not bother most people but it will upset your concentration if you let it get to you. Keep your cool. If your emotions explode, you can be ejected and your team must play a substitute. If you let your anger take over, you are not focused on the game.

Likewise in Life. There are always aggressors, people who try to anger you for no reason. These people are usually unhappy for some other reason but take their anger out on you. The solution is to ignore them and stay focused on your own work. When you allow their provocation to anger you, you are the weak one.

nd whatever you do, whether in word or deed, do it all in the name of the Lord Jesus, giving thanks to God the Father through him.

Col. 3:17

Play a Second Sport

Playing more than one sport can benefit an athlete tremendously. The hand-eye coordination gained on the second string basketball team can be of assistance to the starting fullback on the football team. Being well rounded exposes a player to new and diverse playing tactics.

Likewise in Life. The manufacturing person who spends time with the sales division will understand customers desires. The vice president who spends a day on the phone in customer service will be reminded of the daily rigors faced by those in less prestigious roles, and better understand the company's customers.

If we are distressed, it is for your comfort and salvation.... And our hope for you is firm, because we know that just as you share in our sufferings, so also you share in our comfort.

2 Corinthians 1:6-7

Develop the Proper Attitude

In any sport there are winners and there are losers. A good competitor maintains his dignity even after a loss. The best athletes never give up. After a loss, they practice even harder and return ready to win.

Likewise in Life. You may lose a sale, or make a mistake that can cost you. It is not whether you lose, but how you respond to your failure. To not care is a sign of giving up. A winner cares deeply, accepts a loss with dignity, and resolves to succeed next time.

Follow the Shot

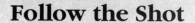

Just about half of the shots in basketball are missed. Once the ball leaves the player's hands, it is a free ball. When the shot is taken, everyone must be ready to grab the rebound.

Likewise in Life. We do not always get what we want on the first try. The person who is persistent stays involved and does not give up too early, is more likely to achieve his goal on a later try. When persistence becomes a habit, success becomes a matter of time ... sooner or later success will happen.

is purpose was to create in himself one new man out of the two, thus making peace, and in this one body to reconcile both of them to God through the cross, by which he put to death their hostility.

Ephesians 2:15-16

Two Talents Complement Each Other

In sports it is important to be a competent player with both hands. Being able to dribble with either hand makes you a much more versatile basketball player. A batter who can switch-hit can adjust to today's pitcher.

Likewise in Life. In business it can be important—sometimes even necessary— to speak two languages, or give a presentation while drawing graphs. Being multi-talented opens new doors and can increase your effectiveness and your value.

I guide you in the way of wisdom and lead you along
straight paths. When you walk, your steps will not be hampered;
when you run, you will not stumble. Hold on to instruction,
do not let it go; guard it well, for it is your life.

Proverbs 4:11-13

Mental Preparation

Every athletic event has physical and mental challenges. Most people do not realize how much mental discipline it takes to exceed at a high level. Great athletes know what they are going to do before it happens. They mentally rehearse the movements so many times, they can respond physically with ease.

Likewise in Life. It is not enough to be physically fit to go the distance at work. You must also stay mentally fit: reading industry news, learning new programs willingly. Eventually, every new challenge is met with confidence and mastered.

or where you have envy and selfish ambition, there you find disorder and every evil practice. But the wisdom that comes from heaven is first of all pure; then peace-loving, considerate, submissive, full of mercy and good fruit, impartial and sincere. Peacemakers who sow in peace raise a harvest of righteousness.

James 3:16-18

Turn It On, Turn It Off

On every team there are two opposites: the 'animal' and the 'gentlemen'. The 'animal' talks only of hurting an opponent. Before the game, after the game—it never changes. The 'gentlemen' talks of hard practice, sportsmanship, and the need for teamwork. When the opening whistle blows the 'gentlemen' competes as fiercely as the 'animal'. When the play stops, he is the first to thank the other team for the game.

Likewise in Life. The business world offers people a chance to be classified as animals or gentlemen. Sales quotas, manufacturing targets, and a host of other challenges face you daily. The person who works hard, but remembers that others have feelings, is the MVP of life.

Make it your ambition to lead a quiet life, to mind your own business and to work with your hands, just as we told you, so that your daily life may win the respect of outsiders....

1 Thessalonians 4:11-12

Sweat the Small Stuff

Daily practice of the fundamental skills is the most important part of achievement in any sport. The people who practice hard, play hard. When players arrive at practice early every day, free throw percentages increase, and games are won.

Likewise in Life. A consistent investment in self-improvement can fuel consistent achievement. The small details add up to a big career.

ehold, I will create new heavens and a new earth. The former things will not be remembered, nor will they come to mind.

Isaiah 65:17

Fresh Starts

Every April, the first baseball is thrown out and the regular season begins. Last year's team in the cellar is shooting for this year's pennant. There is fresh grass on the field, new names on the roster, and rekindled enthusiasm among the fans.

Likewise in Life. Whether it's a new job, a new assignment, or a new supervisor– it is a fresh start. Look for those new seasons. Realize the slate is clean and that the year's statistics are just beginning. When you have a new start— seize the opportunity!

*Only let your manner of life be worthy of the gospel of Christ,
so that... I may hear of you that you stand firm in one spirit,
with one mind striving side by side for the faith.*

Philippians 1:27 RSV

The Next Level

The difference between a high school athlete who plays at a higher level and one who does not is practice, leadership and determination. Many good athletes do not make it to the next level because they lack the dedication. Those who go further are the athletes who know what obstacles are ahead at the next level. Determination and hard work are the keys to success in any sport.

Likewise in Life. The competition for high level jobs is fierce. The few who qualify for these positions are the hard workers. They put in the effort necessary for their next job, at their previous job.

Hear, O Israel, today you are going into battle against your enemies. Do not be fainthearted or afraid; do not be terrified or give way to panic before them. For the Lord your God is the one who goes with you to fight for you against your enemies to give you victory.

Deuteronomy 20:3-4

Game Day!

Games are important. Practice is the key to winning—but games are where you win! Without a game all of the practice is only an exercise in exercise.

Likewise in Life. We need to close the sale, win the case, or complete a challenging project to measure our progress and growth. College and academics help prepare you for the real world, but the true test is performance on the job. That is when the preparation yields results.

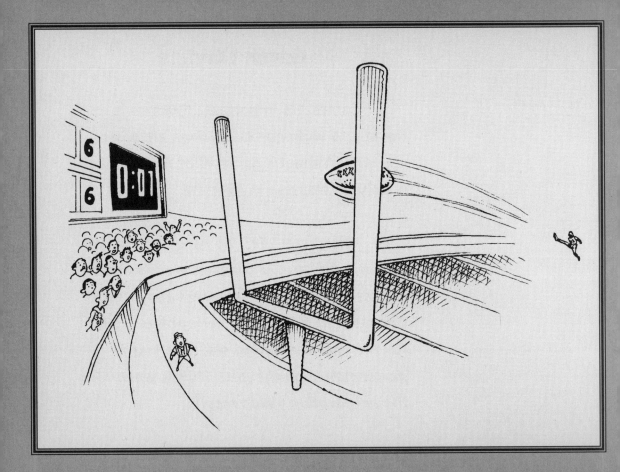

Watch the Clock

In every sport it is inevitable that time will run out. Knowing this, every player should constantly check the clock. The team with the ball when time runs out usually gets the last shot. Sometimes the last shot decides the game.

Likewise in Life. Time is finite so use it wisely, paying attention to deadlines and commitments. Be disciplined with your time and you will be more effective.

And let us consider how we may spur one another on toward love and good deeds. Let us not give up meeting together, as some are in the habit of doing, but let us encourage one another—and all the more as you see the Day approaching.

Hebrews 10:24-25

Know When to Win

There are games in every season that are not important. Win or lose, they do not affect the outcome of the season or the playoff standings. Those are opportunities to work on new techniques, play the second string, and to rest the best players. The crucial games need to be won. In such games the first team must step up and play their hardest.

Likewise in Life. Along the road you will make decisions. Some big, some small, but all have an impact. Leaders know which decisions or projects are critical in the bigger picture. Some are opportunities to test a new idea or a new person, while other projects require the focused effort of the proven team member.

May the God who gives endurance and encouragement give you a spirit of unity among yourselves as you follow Christ Jesus, so that with one heart and mouth you may glorify the God and Father of our Lord Jesus Christ.

Romans. 15:5-6

Teamwork is Half Team and Half Work

People who play well together are considered a team. On a good team, everyone plays off each other and everyone is playing hard. Teams are not created so everyone can do less work. Anyone who is 'taking it easy' will bring down the entire team.

Likewise in Life. Companies do not exist for longer lunch breaks. The combination of good minds and discipline people together enables a project team to succeed. Teams can successfully complete projects that a single person could never do alone.

And we know that in all things God works for the good of those who love him, who have been called according to his purpose.

Romans. 8:28

Sometimes It Is Beyond Your Control

Referees try hard to make the right calls, but sometimes they miss one. Videotape replays occasionally show that the winning touchdown was actually out of bounds, or the runner was tagged out just before he touched the plate. One game might be affected by a bad call, but never a full season.

Likewise in Life. Unfair decisions will that adversely affect each person. Those are the 'bad calls' of life. Take them as they come and continue playing the percentages. The deserving winner will ultimately prevail.

Examine yourselves to see whether you are in the faith; test yourselves. Do you not realize that Christ Jesus is in you—unless, of course, you fail the test? And I trust that you will discover that we have not failed the test.

2 Corinthians 13:5-6

Second Effort

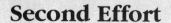

At half-time, our team entered the locker room down by only six points. The coach said: "Every year my best friend and I climb the tallest mountain in California, Mt. Whitney. This mountain is deceiving. The first half of the climb is easy, practically anyone can do it. The second half of the climb is only for those who want to reach the top. Well...we have finished the first half of our climb. Now it's time for the second half. Are you determined to reach the top?"

Likewise in Life. The first half of anything is easy. It is when things get tough, and fatigue sets in, and the competition gets tighter, that the real winners emerge.

I will break down your stubborn pride and make the sky above you like iron and the ground beneath you like bronze.

Leviticus 26:19

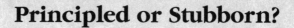

Principled or Stubborn?

Sometimes you are in a short slump and just cannot hit the baseball. If you stay with your swing, you will connect again. That's being principled. If the slump lasts too long, do not be stubborn. Consider changing your swing.

Likewise in Life. If a regimen has worked well in the past—then ride out the slump. Do not allow stubborn pride to keep you stuck in one spot forever. It can be deadly in business. Change your regimen and get back to success.

My son, do not despise the Lord's discipline and do not resent his rebuke, because the Lord disciplines those he loves, as a father the son he delights in.

Proverbs 3:11-12

Mistake-Free

As the season winds down, it is time to review the year. Athletic teams review the year by reflecting on their performances in each game. They are grateful for the victories, but concentrate on the losses, for in the losses are the lessons.

Likewise in Life. Companies look back on the previous year and learn from each experience. Sometimes reviewing past mistakes is painful, but the successful person learns from everything.

Is any man afraid or fainthearted? Let him go home so that his brothers will not become disheartened too.

Deuteronomy 20:8

No Pain, No Gain

In sports, the only way to improve is to struggle through practices, weight-room sessions and tedious drills. Along with enduring the hard work come the benefits of improving in game situations.

Likewise in Life. Many times you will become discouraged or suffer setbacks in your job. You may think it is too hard or not worth it. When your tedious effort is recognized, you realize that without the pain, there is no gain. Keep things in perspective. The gain is worth the pain.

Pick a Sport

There are many sports to choose from. Soccer, basketball, football, lacrosse, baseball, and hockey, to name a few. Without these sports, life would not be as much fun. Sports keep you in shape, as well as develop self-discipline and a spirit of competition. Two or more sports can be played in one season, football and soccer; basketball and soccer; or track and lacrosse. Overlapping sports give more kids a chance to compete.

Likewise in Life. There are many careers to choose from and everyone has a chance to excel if they narrow their focus and devote time to their chosen profession.

Therefore, since we are surrounded by such a great cloud of witnesses, let us throw off everything that hinders and the sin that so easily entangles, and let us run with perseverance the race marked out for us.

Hebrews 12:1.

Time on Task

Fielding grounders, shooting free throws, or practicing footwork, time spent on task is necessary. The more time that is spent on quality practice, the more skilled you become.

Likewise in Life. The so-called experts out there preach: 'work smarter not harder,' and 'quality time not quantity time'. While it is necessary to use time intelligently, be sure to dedicate a sufficient amount of time to master a skill.

imilarly, encourage the young men to be self-controlled. In everything set them an example by doing what is good. In your teaching show integrity, seriousness and soundness of speech that cannot be condemned, so that those who oppose you may be ashamed because they have nothing bad to say about us.

Titus 2:6-8

Cross-Training

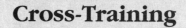

An athlete who competes in only one sport is probably hurting his chances of achieving his maximum potential. Learning from different coaches, playing with different teammates, and developing different moves, can all contribute to overall excellence.

Likewise in Life. Seek opportunities to work outside your own department once in a while. This will develop skills and insight in other areas that will boost your performance in every job classification.

As the rain and the snow come down from heaven, and do not return to it without watering the earth and making it bud and flourish, so that it yields seed for the sower and bread for the eater, so is my word that goes out from my mouth: It will not return to me empty, but will accomplish what I desire and achieve the purpose for which I sent it.

Isaiah 55:9-11

Commitment

To be successful in a sport, you must commit. This must not be a mediocre commitment, but a pledge to give it all you have. Attending practice every day and working out on weekends are all part of the athletic experience.

Likewise in Life. No business wants to hire a person who cannot commit to the efforts of that business. Without a purposeful commitment, your work lacks meaning. With commitment, you become a valuable asset to your team.

o you not know that your body is a temple of the Holy Spirit, who is in you, whom you have received from God? You are not your own; you were bought at a price. Therefore honor God with your body.

1 Corinthians 6:19-20

Recover Quickly

Athletic competition causes injuries. They are nearly impossible to circumvent, but the impact can be minimized by a focused recuperation regimen. With proper therapy, a five-week recovery time might be reduced to two.

Likewise in Life. Everyone in business suffers temporary setbacks. Some are physical, but they can have financial consequences. The important thing is to learn from the experience, and then do everything in your power to get back to business.

have fought the good fight, I have finished the race, I have kept the faith. Now there is in store for me the crown of right-eousness, which the Lord, the righteous Judge, will award to me on that day.

2 Timothy 4:7-8

Do the Drills

Every day during practice you repeat the same drills. This repetition allows you to become accustomed to doing this task, so in a game it is second nature. And repetition builds endurance.

Likewise in Life. Business is full of little details and repeated tasks that are part of a bigger picture, much like mounting the bolts on a car chassis. The best managers understand that the repeated tasks hold the larger projects together.

nd the Lord said, "If as one people speaking the same language they have begun to do this, then nothing they plan to do will be impossible for them."

Genesis 11:6

The Big Game

The Super Bowl matchup is all but decided when the season starts. A team's season merely validates the players' mental preparation, physical aptitude and game-winning focus. If these pieces are in place early in the season, the end result—playing in the Super Bowl—is all but clinched before the first regulation game.

Likewise in Life. The company that offers solid products, attentive customer service, and a knowledgeable sales force is poised for success.

*J*esus replied, "You are in error because you do not know the Scriptures..."

Matthew 22:29

Know the Rules

The athlete who studies the rule book has an advantage. The quarterback in the pocket with no open receivers, about to be sacked, needs to end the play without losing yardage. Intentional grounding is a 10-yard penalty, but passing from within the tackles is a penalty-free grounding. Knowing that important rule allows the quarterback to control the down.

Likewise in Life. Precise rules of procedure and a host of unique standards and specifications exist in every line of work. These details can be the winning difference for the person who uses the rules wisely to his advantage.

But as for you, continue in what you have learned and have become convinced of, because you know those from whom you learned it, and how from infancy you have known the holy Scriptures, which are able to make you wise for salvation through faith in Christ Jesus.

2 Timothy 3:14-15

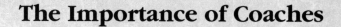

The Importance of Coaches

With every sport there needs to be time set aside for practice. When you practice by yourself, you might be reinforcing bad habits. That is why good coaches are so important. Coaches teach good skills and terminate poor techniques quickly.

Likewise in Life. Never think you know everything and that you must 'do it alone'. The greatest achievements come from people who have mentors to guide and instruct them.

*N*o, in all these things we are more than conquerors through him who loved us. For I am convinced that neither death nor life, neither angels nor demons, neither the present nor the future, nor any powers, neither height nor depth, nor anything else in all creation, will be able to separate us from the love of God that is in Christ Jesus our Lord.

Romans 8:37-39

When Losers Are Winners

Yesterday we played against a team that had beaten us by 28 points in basketball two weeks before. We emerged from the locker room ready to play hard. We played one of our best games. We still lost, but this time by only six points. We worked as a team and followed our game plan. We felt like the real winners because our improvement was so obvious and so tremendous.

Likewise in Life. Achievement is not always gained by huge one-time victories, but in consistent, incremental improvements over time. If we measure and applaud steady improvement, winning will soon follow.

ake every effort to add to your faith goodness; and to goodness, knowledge; and to knowledge, self-control; and to self-control, perseverance... kindness and love. For if you possess these qualities... they will keep you from being ineffective and unproductive...

2 Peter 1:5-7

Catch, Then Run

An inexperienced punt or kickoff receiver will sometimes begin to run before he has caught the football. With many defenders rushing towards him, the result is almost always a fumble, loss of possession, and good field position for the opponent. It is very costly to begin running before you have a firm hand on the ball.

Likewise in Life. A person may strive to accomplish a distant goal, when it is the more immediate task that needs attention. Get the small things done first, and the larger, more visible successes will follow.

TOPICAL INDEX

Note:

Note:

Note:

Note:

_____

_____

_____

_____

_____

_____

_____

Note:

_____

_____

_____

_____

_____

_____

_____

Note: